# FIRST PHOTOS

## How *Kids* Can Take *Great* Pictures

BY ART EVANS

# FIRST PHOTOS

## How *Kids* can Take *Great* Pictures

### BY ART EVANS

ISBN 0-9626508-7-0

Library of Congress Catalog Card Number 92-50482

Library of Congress Cataloging in Publication Data
Evans, Arthur G.
   First photos : how kids can take great pictures/by Art Evans
      p. cm.
      Summary: An introduction to basic picture taking for ages eight to twelve.
      ISBN 0-9626508-7-0 : $9.95
      Photography—Juvenile literature. [1. Photography.]
1. Title
TR149.E94 1992
771—dc20                                                         92-50482
                                                                    CIP
                              AC

Published by Photo Data Research
800-8 South Pacific Coast Highway, Redondo Beach, California 90277
Phone (310) 543-1085, Fax (310) 540-8068
Distributed by Login Publishers Consortium (800) 626-4330

Edited by Dorothy Clendenin
Electronic document assembly and color separations by Jim Plowden
Thanks to Martin, David, Peter and Alice Evans and to their mother, Alicia. Thanks also to Ginny Dixon and David Evans and especially to Anne Sharp.
Photography by Matthew Brady, Alicia Evans, Art Evans, Peter Evans, Peter Gowland and Anne Sharp.

Printed in Canada

# FIRST PHOTOS

**A Photo Data Research Book**

# Contents

## Chapter 1

# PHOTOGRAPHY

**This portrait of President Abraham Lincoln was made by Matthew Brady, one of the most famous photographers at the time of the American Civil War. It was made in black and white on a glass plate. Color photography was a novelty in 1860. Because of the pictures made by Brady and others, the War Between the States was the first time the horrors of war were recorded for history.**

Photography is almost like magic. With a camera, you can freeze a moment in time. The word *photograph* is from the Greek words *photo*, meaning *light*, and *graph*, which means *to draw* or *write*. A photograph is *drawing with light*.

You may keep your favorite photos all your life. Pictures you take now, you may give to your own children some day. Your children may keep them for their children. Photos are among the most important personal belongings we own.

You can keep a record of exciting things that happen, make pictures of your family, friends, pets, home, parties, and trips—in fact, almost anything you can see!

Take a photograph of your mother now, and every time you look at her picture, you will remember your mother as she was the day you took her picture.

On this page is a portrait of President Abraham Lincoln. Even though this photograph was taken more than 130 years ago, we know exactly what he looked like at the time he became President of the United States. Somehow, almost by magic, we can tell what kind of person he was.

Would you like to take pictures people will see and enjoy many years from now? If you practice, and learn from this book, you can take great pictures.

**There are three different brands of one-time cameras: Kodak, Fuji, and Konica. They look a little different, but they all work the same way. Each will take satisfactory photographs. When you learn how, you will be able to take great pictures with them.**

You may have heard someone say, "That camera takes good pictures." This is like saying "That shovel digs good holes," or, "This pencil writes good letters." *People* dig holes and write letters. Shovels and pencils are just tools, and so are cameras. You can take great pictures with the simplest cameras. The key is you, not the camera.

You may think that making good pictures is expensive and difficult. Not so.

As in almost everything that people do, there are things you can learn to do that will make your pictures look better. As for cost, a camera that takes 24 pictures can cost less than ten dollars, and you can buy one almost anywhere.

Some people call this type of camera a disposable camera, because it is used only one time. When you take it to a photo lab to have your pictures printed, they will return the camera to the manufacturer to be used again. A better name for them is, "One-time camera."

One-time cameras come with film already inside. You don't have to put the film into the camera or take it out. After you have shot all the pictures, you take

**Sisters, brothers and pets make good subjects for great photos. If this was your sister with your family dog, what do you think you could do with it? For an answer, look at the end of this chapter.**

the camera to a place that develops and prints the film. Some photo stores can finish your pictures in one hour. This usually costs about twice as much as other places where it takes a day, or more, to get your photos back.

Even a simple camera is not a toy. Here are some guidelines to help you take good care of your camera:

1. Keep it dry. Don't let it get wet or damp. Water will ruin both the camera and film.

2. Keep it cool. Unless you are using it, keep it out of the sun. Don't leave a camera in a locked car, the heat will ruin the film.

3. Keep it clean. Sand, dirt, or dust can hurt your camera.

**Photography stores like this can be found almost anywhere. They sell one-time cameras and film. They also develop and print pictures in one hour, or in some cases, even less than one hour.**

**Do you have a pet? If so, take some pictures of your pet the first time you shoot. To get one good picture, take more than one shot. Take at least three, maybe more. After you see your pictures, you may think you can do better. If so, shoot some more. Having a really good picture of your pet will be very important to you when you are older.**

4. Keep it safe. Don't drop it, or bang it around. It may break.

As soon as you finish shooting the pictures, take the camera or film for developing and printing. If you keep the film too long without having it developed, the colors on the film will fade.

We will show you how to use a one-time camera, but all cameras work pretty much the same way.

If you don't already have a camera to use, you may want to buy one of the one-time cameras shown on page 6.

**ANSWER: How about giving a print in a frame to your mother for her birthday? Why not mail a copy to your grandparents? For sure you would want to put a print in your family photo album, wouldn't you?**

# Chapter 2

# YOUR FIRST CAMERA

You can buy a one-time camera almost anywhere: a supermarket, a department store, drugstore or variety store. Some people like to shop at a camera store because the people who work there know about photography and will be able to help you and answer your questions.

When you get to a store, you will find that there are five different kinds of one-time cameras. The least expensive is just a camera. Another model has a flash, another can be used under water, while others take wide pictures or have a telephoto lens for taking pictures far away. The best camera to start with is just the camera alone.

When you buy something new, what is the first thing to do? If you answered, "read the directions," you are right.

With cameras, reading the directions is very important because all cameras are not the same. If you don't follow the directions carefully, your pictures may not come out the way you want them to. They may not come out at all!

First, read everything on the box. Some of the words are advertising, but there is also important information. For instance, do you see the words "24 exposures" or "24 exposure film?" What do you think this means? If you thought that when you use this camera, you can take 24 pictures with it, you were correct.

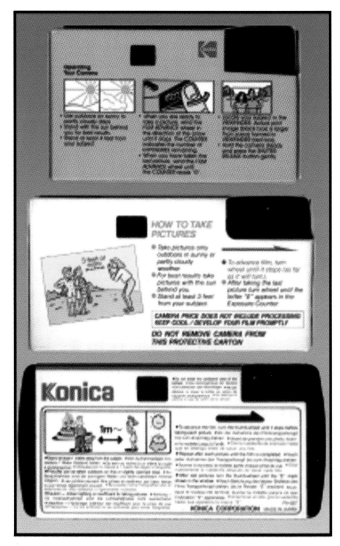

Every one-time camera comes with instructions printed on the back. Be sure to read the instructions carefully before you start to use a camera. The instructions may be a little different on different one-time cameras, so be sure to read the instructions every time you buy a new one.

**The instructions tell you that if you take a picture with the camera too close, it will be out of focus. This is what a photograph looks like when it is out of focus.**

Pay particular attention to the directions on the camera that tell you how to take pictures. Keep reading this part over and over until you know it by heart. You should know the directions well enough so you can operate the camera without thinking about it. To take great pictures, you will have other things to think about.

If you are not using a one-time camera, you will have to learn how to load and unload the film. Also you will have to learn to operate the camera. When you start, it is best to use as simple a camera as possible.

Take the foil-wrapped camera out of the box and remove the camera from the foil. Be sure to put the box and the foil in a trash container. Don't be a litter bug!

The camera is made of plastic and covered with cardboard. A lot of the cardboard is covered with printing. The directions on how to use the camera are written on the cardboard.

Don't try to start taking pictures yet. Sit down and quietly read everything on the camera. There is a lot of little type, so you have to be patient.

Some of the writing tells you how to use the camera, other things are important information and still other words are just advertising. One thing it always says on a one-time camera is "Do Not Open." If you open up the camera, it will be ruined. The film in the camera cannot be exposed to light. If light is allowed to it the film will be ruined.

**What do you think happened in this picture? Look at the end of this chapter for the answer.**

Before you load a camera, you have to buy film. It doesn't matter what brand you buy. All of them will take pictures. Whether or not the picture is great depends on you.

To learn with this book, you should buy color negative film with a speed of 400. Somewhere on the package, it will say "ISO 400." It will also say "color print film" or "color negative." You can choose how many pictures you can take on a roll: 12, 24 or 36. Most one-time cameras are loaded with 24-exposure film.

Each camera is a little different, so you'll have to read the directions to find out exactly how to load and unload the film. If you don't have the directions, you will have to ask someone who knows how, to show you. If nobody you know can help, a clerk at a camera store is usually happy to teach you how, especially if you buy the film there.

There are a few rules for every camera. When the film is not in the camera, keep it in a cool, dry place.

**As soon as you get your pictures back, study all of them carefully. One way to better photography is to look for ways to improve your pictures. You may want to keep a book of examples for future reference.**

When you load and unload your camera, do it in shady or dim light. Avoid direct sunlight. Get your film processed as soon as possible after taking it out of the camera. Always keep your camera very clean, safe, cool and dry. If it has a case, use it. If it has a cap for the lens, use that too.

**ANSWER: The instructions on the camera said, "Stand at least 4 feet from your subject." The boy is 4 feet away, but the dog is closer and out of focus. Make sure everything you want to be in focus is at least 4 feet away (or with some other one-time cameras, 3 feet).**

**When you go to buy film, have in mind what you want. To start out, buy 24-exposure 400 ISO color print film.**

**Chapter 3**

# HOW TO HOLD IT

The way you hold a camera is very important. The rule to remember: Always hold it as steady as you can. If the camera is not steady when you take a picture, the photograph will not be sharp. It will look fuzzy or blurred.

From reading Chapter 2 and the directions on the camera, you already know how to take a picture: Push the shutter release button. The way you push the shutter release is very important.

**Always make sure that one of your fingers is not covering the lens.**

**What is wrong with this picture and why? To find the answer, look at the end of this chapter.**

You already know that when you want to take a picture, you hold the camera in front of your face and look through the little hole to see what the photograph will look like. Look at the front of the camera and you will see a small lens. This is what takes the picture. As you hold the camera, you must always make very sure that none of your fingers are covering the lens. If you get your finger—or anything else—in front of the lens, your picture will not come out.

Hold the camera with your left hand. Your thumb should be on the bottom and your forefinger on top. Look at the picture on page 13, so you'll get it right the first time.

**This is what your pictures will look like if your finger is even a little in front of the lens.**

Use your right hand to push the shutter release. Actually, you don't push, you squeeze. Put your forefinger on the shutter release and your thumb on the bottom of the camera. To take a picture, slowly squeeze your finger and thumb together.

If there is any movement, the picture will not be as sharp as it would have been if the camera were perfectly still. Do you think you can hold the camera perfectly still while you squeeze your finger and thumb together? To get better at it, practice squeezing before you roll the film to the first picture. This way, you won't waste film while you practice.

Did you say you could keep the camera perfectly still?

If you said yes, you were wrong. Even when we try to be very still, we are moving. Our heart is beating and we are breathing. So no matter how hard we try, we cannot be perfect. And obviously, if you are laughing or talking, you are not still.

Many photographers don't even try to hold a camera. They find something to put it on. Whenever you take pictures, think about keeping the camera as still as possible. When you decide to take a picture, look around and see if there might be something you can put it on.

If you can find some way to brace yourself, you will take better pictures. Look around and see if there is something to lean on, or brace yourself against.

**Practice putting your thumb and fingers in the proper position.**

Do you remember the two things that make you move even when you think you are still? Breathing and your heart beating. If you could eliminate one of these, your pictures will be sharper. You can't stop your heart from beating, but you can hold your breath. The best way to do this is to take a deep breath, let half out, hold it and squeeze your finger and thumb together.

Don't expect to be able to do this immediately. It takes some practice. Take a lot of pretend pictures so you don't waste film while you learn. Every time you do it, concentrate. Hold the camera with your left hand, forefinger on top, thumb on the bottom. Put your right forefinger on the shutter release and your right thumb on the bottom. If possible, brace yourself against something. Take a deep breath. Let half out and hold it.

Squeeze your finger and thumb together.

Did you know that this method of taking pictures is something of a secret? A lot of people who take pictures all the time don't know this secret. The result is that a lot of their pictures are never really sharp. Now you know the secret. So use it, every time.

After you take a picture, always wind the knob so you will be ready to take another picture. It is very discouraging to pick up your camera to take a picture and it won't go click. After you take each picture, look at the counter. It tells you how many pictures are left to take.

Don't forget to practice a lot. Photography is a skill, just like writing or playing ball. The more you do it, the better you get. But when you practice, be sure that you are always practicing the right way.

**The steadier you hold the camera, the sharper your picture will be.**

Every time you pick up your camera to take a picture, think of the things you have to do. As the picture is being taken, the camera must be still. Hold the camera with both hands. Use your right hand to take the picture and your left hand to steady the camera. Put you forefinger on top of the camera and your thumb on the bottom. Make sure your forefinger is on the shutter release button. Take a deep breath, let half out and hold it. Squeeze your right thumb and forefinger together.

If possible, find something to lean on and steady yourself as you take a picture. Look around and find things you can put the camera on instead of holding it.

It's easy to take sharp pictures.

**ANSWER: The picture is out of focus or blurred. The reason is that the camera was not still enough when the picture was taken. Practice holding your camera as still as possible.**

# Chapter 4

# KEEP IT LEVEL

Have you ever seen a picture where the things in it look like they are falling over, or seem to be going down hill?

You would never take a picture like this, would you? Of course not. You may not want to, but it is very easy to make this mistake. Every time you take a picture, you have to think about preventing this problem.

The way you do it is to keep the camera level. Actually, what you do is keep everything level as you look in the viewfinder. What you see in the viewfinder is what the picture will look like.

There are certain things we take pictures of that we have to keep level.

**If you hold your camera like this, your pictures will look like some of those in this chapter. Always check to make sure your camera is level.**

**What do you think is wrong with this picture and why? Look at the end of this chapter for the answer.**

The most important is the ocean or a lake we can't see across. The line of the water must be parallel to the top of the viewfinder. Otherwise the ocean will look as if it is pouring off the edge of the earth.

We have to use this same rule when we take a picture of the earth at a distance. The line where the earth meets the sky must be parallel to the top of the viewfinder.

There are other things we take pictures of that have to be level. Buildings, for instance. When you take a picture of your house or apartment, be sure that the edge of the building is parallel to one side of the viewfinder.

**A tilted picture of the ocean looks really strange.**

**When you take a picture of the ocean, make sure the top of your viewfinder is parallel with the horizon line. The horizon is the line where the Earth meets the sky.**

Take a picture of your home. You probably won't live there all your life and you'll want to be able to remember what it looked like.

Can you think of some other things that have to be level in the viewfinder? How about a picture of someone standing in a door, or sitting at a table?

**If you do not hold the camera straight, objects will seem to lean to the right or left, or seem to be falling away from the camera.**

**To take a picture like this, make sure that the pole and the sides of the house are parallel with the sides of your viewfinder.**

Do your parents have a car? Cars are something important to many of us. So why not take a picture of it? Does it have to be level? What should you look for on the car to keep parallel to a side of the viewfinder?

Every time you take a picture, concentrate on keeping the camera level. Certain things in the viewfinder must be parallel with a side of the viewfinder. If you are even a little bit off, the picture will look strange.

Even when there are no straight lines in the scene you see in your viewfinder, you still have to keep the camera level. Think about a picture of a person:

if you tilt the camera even a little, the photograph may look strange.

When you pick up your camera to take a picture, don't just go snap. Study what you see in the viewfinder. Look for things that should be parallel to a side of the viewfinder. Remember how you should hold your camera. Take a breath and let half out. Squeeze your finger and thumb together to take the picture.

**ANSWER: The camera was tilted when the picture was taken. How can you tell? Look at the telephone poles at the top of the hill. Look at the lifeguard station.**

# Chapter 5

# LONG OR TALL

When you look in the viewfinder of your camera, the shape you see that outlines the scene is a rectangle.

Most photographs are rectangles. They are not square. Can you tell what a rectangle is? You have probably studied this during math at school.

You can hold your camera different ways. One way you can take a picture is with the rectangle longer than it is tall.

The other way, the rectangle is taller than it is long.

Look in your viewfinder and try it both ways. Look at a number of different scenes both ways. Try a person standing, try a person's face, try a pet, try a building, try a distant scene like mountains or hills.

Of course, there are more than these two choices. You could twist your camera any which way. But, if you do, what happens to the level rules we learned about in Chapter 4?

When you take a picture, you have to choose whether the photograph will be long or tall.

**If you hold your camera like this . . .**

**The picture will look like this.**

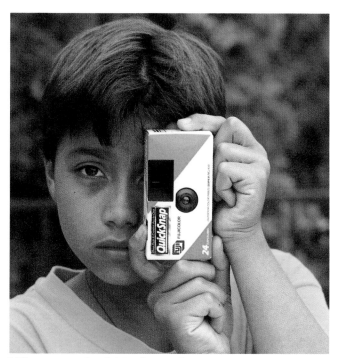

**When you hold it the other way . . .**

**The picture comes out like this.**

Photographers call this choice, "format." Format is a good word to learn.

A photographer taking a tall picture says that it has a vertical format. The photograph will be taller than it is long. A photographer taking a long picture says that it has a horizontal format. Do you already know these words: format, horizontal, vertical?

**What do you think about the format used for this picture? For the answer, look at the end of this chapter.**

Most things you take pictures of look better one way or the other. If you are taking a person's face, a portrait, should the picture be long or tall? Let's try to say it a better way. Should the format be horizontal or vertical? Most photographers use a vertical format for portraits. The photograph is usually more pleasing this way.

Most people—even adults—take most of their pictures using a horizontal format. The reason for this is that cameras are easier to hold and operate this way. But most people don't take great pictures. They just take ordinary snapshots. Every time you take a picture, try to imagine which format will look best.

Do you want to take great pictures, or

**The picture on the left was taken in the vertical format. It is taller than it is wide. Most pictures of a person look better if you use the vertical format.**

photographers take more vertical than horizontal pictures. This is just the opposite of almost everyone else, isn't it?

Don't be horizontal all the time. Everything you take pictures of looks better one way or the other. The format is another thing you need to think about every time you pick up your camera.

Now when you take pictures, remember the right way to hold the camera, keep it level and decide whether the format should be long or tall, horizontal or vertical. As you take the picture, brace yourself, take a deep breath, let half out, hold it and squeeze your finger and thumb together.

Do you remember what to do after you take a picture? Wind the film so the camera is ready again, right?

And when you are through shooting, put your camera away in a safe, dry, cool place.

ordinary snapshots? You probably answered great pictures or you wouldn't be reading this book.

Look in some magazines and study the work of professional photographers. Are all of the pictures in a horizontal format? One of the secrets of taking great pictures is making the choice between horizontal and vertical every time you look in your viewfinder.

Actually, many professional

**ANSWER: The rule is that you should use a vertical format when taking a picture of a person's face. But in photography, all rules are made to be broken. In this case, the boy is posed in such a way that a horizontal format is best.**

**Chapter 6**

# WATCH THE LIGHT

The reason we can see is because there is light. This is the same with a camera. If there is no light, there can be no photographs.

When there is not much light, it is very difficult for us to see clearly. Cameras are like this too. If there is too little light, photographs will not be satisfactory.

Most cameras need more light than we do. When the light is dim, we can often see when a camera cannot take a picture. For a camera to operate properly, there has to be enough light.

How do you know when enough is enough? There are many different kinds of cameras and different kinds of film.

**This picture was taken at dusk. The sun was still out, but it was almost down. You can see the result.**

But the basic one-time camera you are using needs sunlight.

To use the basic one-time camera, the sun has to be out and you have to be outside. You cannot use this camera to take pictures at night or inside.

If you are outside and there are clouds covering the sun, you can still take pictures.

If the sun is out and you want to take a picture of something in the shade, the camera will still work.

If there is a storm or very dark clouds, there may not be enough light. (But this is an interesting time to shoot, so you might want to try it anyway. Just be sure not to get your camera wet.) If it is cloudy and you are trying to shoot something in a dark, shady place, there may not be enough light.

So now, every time you get ready to take a picture, you have to ask yourself, is there enough light?

The sun is where the light comes from, but it can be a problem too. What happens if you try to look directly at the sun? If you answered, "I should never look directly at the sun," you know an important health rule. If we look directly at the sun, the light will hurt our eyes.

If you point your camera directly at the sun and take a picture, the photograph will not come out. The light from the sun is too strong for the film.

This picture was taken on an overcast day. What do you think about the result?

This picture was taken on a sunny day. Compare the shadows on the two girls' faces with the one taken on an overcast day. What do you think is a good rule when taking pictures of people? For the answer, look at the end of this chapter.

Even if you are not pointing the camera directly at the sun, if you can see the sun in your viewfinder, there will be a problem. The best rule for now is: Keep the sun out of the picture. When you become more advanced, you can learn how to take pictures that include the sun. But you will need a different camera. The one-time camera cannot do it.

What do the directions say about the sun? They tell you to keep the sun at your back as you take pictures. This is a safe rule and if you follow it, your pictures will always come out.

But there are times when we cannot get the sun at our back and there are others where the scene looks better with the sun somewhere else.

Go out in the sun and hold your camera so that the rays of the sun hit the lens. Observe how this looks.

Then take one hand and place it between the lens and the sun. The glass looks different, doesn't it?

The rule is, keep the rays of the sun from striking the lens. If you want to take a picture and the sun is striking the lens, you have to shade it somehow. One way to do this is to stand in a place where something provides shade. Or you can ask someone to use their hand as a shade. Some very advanced photographers can hold the camera and take the picture with one hand and use their other hand for a shade.

Now there are more and more things to think about every time you take a picture. To make this work, you will have to memorize the things to do. It isn't that easy. This is why some people take great pictures and almost everyone else does not.

**Look at the picture of the boy. Where is the sun coming from? Was this a good position to take the picture from?**

**Look at the shadow of the boy. Where is the sun? Was this a good place to stand to take the picture?**

Can you review the things you have to do?

1.  Is the film wound and the camera ready to shoot?

2.  Watch the light.

3.  Decide whether the format should be long or tall.

4.  Level things in the viewfinder.

5.  Hold the camera correctly.

6.  Brace yourself.

7.  Take a deep breath, let half out and hold it.

8.  Squeeze your finger and thumb together.

9.  Wind the film so the camera is ready again.

10. Put it away in a safe, dry, cool place.

**ANSWER: Faces often photograph better when the sky is overcast or when the people are in the shade. The harsh shadows from direct sunlight don't usually make a pleasing people picture.**

# Chapter 7

# POINT OF VIEW

When you take a picture, you decide where the camera will be at the moment you squeeze your finger and thumb together. There are thousands of places the camera could be, but you have selected a single one.

Imagine that you are about to take a picture of a person sitting in a chair. How many places could you position the camera to take the picture? You could walk all around and take the picture anywhere on the circle. You could get down on your hands and knees and crawl around the circle. You could get on a step ladder and keep moving it around the circle. And you could make the circle larger or smaller, thus positioning the camera closer or farther away.

You could even dig a hole, get down in it with your camera and shoot up. Or you could get in a balloon and shoot straight down. When you think about it, there is an almost unlimited number of choices. When you take a picture, you have to pick a single point to shoot from. You place the camera at this point and look through the viewfinder at your subject.

There is one thing you can't do, however, and that is get too close. What do the instructions say? If you have forgotten, pick up your camera and read them again. You have to be at least 3 or 4 feet away from your subject.

**When you take a picture like this, you will want to use as close a point of view as possible. But if you get too close, your picture will be out of focus. Using a stick is a good way to make sure you don't get too close. Check the directions to see if you should use a 3 or a 4-foot stick.**

(3 or 4 feet depending on the kind of one-time camera you are using.) To help you remember how far 3 feet is, get a yard stick. Practice holding it between your face and different objects.

Photographers call the position of the camera the "point of view." To think about and understand this idea is very important for you to be able to take great pictures. Some photographers believe that for any one subject, there is a single best point of view.

**Compare the point of view in the picture on the left with the one on the right. Most great pictures are taken from a "tight" point of view. This means that the picture is taken from such a close point that everything not necessary is not in the photograph.**

Every picture ever taken was shot from a single point of view. This point was chosen by the person operating the camera. How good, bad, ordinary or great the picture is depends a lot on the point of view.

To take a picture, most people just pick up a camera and snap away without thinking much about the point of view. One of the secrets of being able to take great pictures is thinking about selecting an interesting, revealing or unusual point of view.

Most people take pictures while standing in front of the subject. So most pictures taken by adults are from a point of view between 5 and 6 feet off the ground. When children take pictures, the point of view may be lower.

And when professional basketball players take pictures, the point of view will be very much higher.

**Many people shoot their pets from a looking down position. The pet is on the floor and the photographer is standing up. But if you get on the same level as your pet, you will have a much better chance of getting a great picture.**

**What is it about this picture that makes it a little different from other pictures of kids playing? Look at the end of the chapter for the answer.**

When you take a picture and show it to someone, this is a communication, just as if you had written or talked.

Every time you take a picture, think about what you are trying to communicate. There are all sorts of communications. Here are a few examples: What a beautiful sunset! This is what Jack looked like when he was 10 years old. Alice got a Barbie doll for Christmas. This is the house we lived in when I was 12.

Each picture makes some sort of statement or communication. How many times have you seen a picture which says, "I'm confused; I don't know what I am trying to communicate?"

When you have decided exactly what you want to communicate, then you can select the best point of view. To decide, you have to look. And you have to concentrate while you look.

Remember the choices: You can get close or you can get far away. You can get high or you can get low. And you can walk all around. When you decide to take a photograph, walk all about and really look.

Most pictures have the same sort of look because they are all taken at the same height off the ground. And if something is always the same, what is it? Boring!

Writing is a way to communicate. Can you think of another way we use every day? How about talking? Making a photo is also a way to communicate.

Now that you have learned about the idea of point of view, don't expect that the idea will enable you to take great pictures right away. You will probably take better pictures than most people. But to take great pictures, you will have to practice. This means selecting a point of view, taking a picture, getting the print back and studying the result.

Peter Gowland

This picture was taken from a low angle. Imagine what it would look like if it were taken while the photographer was standing.

A picture will not look the same as the scene did to your eyes. A picture has no depth. It is rectangular and flat. So when you select a point of view, you need to visualize it rectangular and flat.

Here is a review of the things to do:

1. Make sure the camera is ready to shoot.

2. Select a point of view.

3. Decide what the format should be.

4. Keep things level in the viewfinder.

5. Hold the camera correctly and brace yourself.

6. Take a deep breath, let half out and hold it.

7. Squeeze your finger and thumb together.

8. Wind the film so the camera is ready for the next picture.

9. Put the camera away. Where and how? If you don't remember, look on the last page of chapter 6.

**ANSWER: The shot was taken from a high angle looking down on the equipment and the kids. From this angle, the photo shows the kids' faces as they enjoy their play. A photograph of the same thing taken from the usual person-height point of view would not have been nearly as interesting. Always look for the unusual or revealing point of view.**

**Chapter 8**

# COMPOSITION

Do you know what the word "composition" means? It comes from the word "compose." If you look in a dictionary, it says, "To make or form by combining things, parts or elements."

**Do you think this picture was just taken or do you think it was arranged or directed? For the answer, look at the end of this chapter.**

Look at any picture. Isn't it formed by arranging things within the edges of the photo? There is almost always more than one thing in a photograph. How the things are arranged in a picture is called composition. To have a great picture, you need a great composition.

There are two different ways of taking a photograph. One way is to take things as they are. Another is to arrange things the way you want them before you take the picture.

Let's suppose you want to take a picture of your cat or dog. Your pet is just lying there, so you pick up your camera and make sure it is ready to shoot, select a good point of view, choose the format, check your level and squeeze off a shot.

Another way would be to study your pet. Notice what color it is. Then find something with a contrasting color. If you have a tan and white dog, you might want to place it on a red rug. Now you have arranged things differently than they were. Colors are part of the composition and you have selected contrasting colors to improve the composition.

Let's further suppose that after you look at the dog on the red rug, the scene doesn't look too interesting. You don't want just an ordinary picture, you want a great one.

So you find a toy car. With a little persuasion, you get your dog to sit in the car while you take the picture. Now you have introduced another thing into the composition.

A composition is made up of things. Each thing has a shape and a color or a combination of colors. The way you arrange these things, by changing your point of view or by adding, subtracting or moving things around, changes the composition.

Ever since there was art, artists have studied composition. It has been found that certain compositions are more pleasing to most people than others. Study paintings, drawings and photographs. Look at the way artists arrange things. What do you like? What don't you like?

**This picture was taken inside with a flash camera. To learn how you can take one like this, be sure to read the next chapter as soon as you finish this one.**

Over the years, artists have developed rules of composition. Of course, since photography is art, the rules are not hard and fast like those in math or grammar. But they do provide us with things to think about when we take pictures.

There are many rules, but, for now, we'll only learn a few. As you know, to take great pictures you have a lot of other things to remember too.

Many ordinary pictures can be made into great pictures by using three rules: thirds, frame and lead-in. You'll want to memorize these: thirds, frame, lead-in.

A photograph is a rectangle. The rectangle on this page is divided into thirds. If you arrange compositions so the shapes of things fall along the thirds lines, it will probably be more pleasing.

Try to frame the subjects of your pictures. A frame is a thing closer to you than your subject. An example of a frame is a picture of a mountain with a tree on one side and branches on the top.

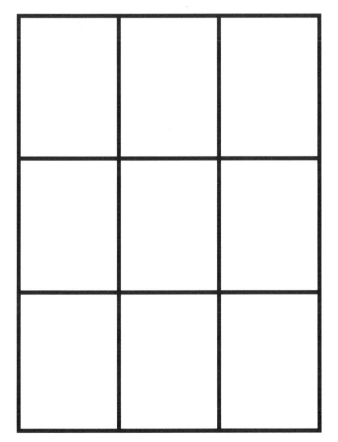

**To see how the ⅓ rule works, draw lines on a rectangle.**

**The tree provides a frame for the church. Imagine the rectangle divided into thirds on this picture. How does it come out?**

You should apply the lead-in rule even when nothing is moving. If someone is looking in a direction, compose the picture so that there is more space in front of the look than in back. There are all sorts of ways you can use the lead-in rule.

By now, you have learned a lot. There was a lot to learn, wasn't there? You have to know how to operate your camera, how to hold it, keep it level, choose a format, watch the light and select a point of view. Now you are adding composition.

At this point, many people think that if only they had a better camera, they could take great pictures.

You probably know people who have expensive and complicated cameras. Those who make and sell cameras try to convince us that if we buy a better camera, we will take better pictures. But here is a secret that every professional photographer knows: You don't need a fancy, expensive and complicated camera to take good pictures or even great pictures. What you do need, however, are the things you are learning in this book. Many professional photographers use simpler and less expensive cameras than do amateurs.

When you shoot, think about leading in. What does this mean? Take the example of someone running. When you look in your viewfinder, where should you place the runner? In the middle? No. Place the runner so that there is more space in front of the runner than in back. Now let's carry this rule a little farther. Try to place the runner on the one-third line. When you take your picture, follow the runner with your camera.

How many rules can you see applied in this picture? You can probably see thirds both ways, but the curve of the beach leads you into the picture. Shapes can lead in as well as motion.

Notice that there is more room in front of the girl than behind her. This makes it seem as though she is running into the picture. Also notice that she is about on the ⅓ line.

The things you have learned can be applied to any camera. But there isn't any camera that will hold itself, keep itself level, choose its own format, watch the light, select a point of view and compose the shapes and colors.

Every time you use your camera, plan carefully. Try to imagine a picture in your head that will show what the actual picture will look like.

ANSWER: Although it may look casual, this picture was arranged or directed. It would be very difficult to just snap a picture and get a result like this. The boy was directed exactly where and when to walk. The point of view and format were carefully selected beforehand.

# Chapter 9

# USE THE FLASH

Remember the chapter on watching the light? What did you learn about when and where you can take pictures? Only during the daytime, right? Without the sun, there isn't enough light.

There is a way you can take pictures at night or inside. You can use a flash. If you are using one-time cameras, you will have to buy a one-time camera with a built-in flash. It will cost a few dollars more than the one without it.

If you are using another kind of camera, you will have to use one with a built-in flash or one that you can attach a separate flash.

**When you buy a one-time camera with a flash, look at the box carefully to be sure you have the right one.**

The one-time flash camera is different. What is the first thing you do when you get a new or different camera? Read the directions, right?

The flash is something photographers call an accessory. This means that it is there when you need it, but you don't have to use it unless you want to. Just because you have a camera with a flash doesn't mean that you have to use it for every picture. You only use it when it will help you make a better picture.

What are the times when you need flash? Obviously, when there is not enough light. If the sun is down, you can assume you need the flash. If you are shooting inside, you also need the flash.

The flash is very bright, but not nearly as strong as the sun. The light from the flash only works for a short distance. Things you want to take pictures of can be no farther than 10 feet from a one-time camera. Other cameras and flashes may be different, so if you are not using a one-time camera, be sure to read the directions carefully.

To use a one-time camera with flash, before you can take a picture, you have to push a button and wait for a little light to come on. The little light—called a ready-light—means that the flash is ready. Most other types of cameras and flashes have a similar light. If you forget to wait for the ready-light, the flash will not go off and your picture will be too dark.

Remember the chapter on holding your camera? One of the important things you learned was to be careful not to get your finger in front of the lens. When you use a camera with flash, there are two things not to get your finger in front of: the lens and the flash. Practice with your camera so that you can hold it without getting your fingers in the way. You need to practice enough so this becomes automatic.

Look directly at the front of your camera. Notice that the flash is on one side and the lens on another. You need to remember that the flash is on the side of the camera you hold with your left hand.

Here is an important rule: When you want to take a vertical (tall) format picture, the left side of the camera should be up. This way, the flash will be above the lens. Photographs appear more pleasing when the light comes from above.

The light from the flash is just like any other light. The closer you are, the brighter it is. To put it another way, the brightness decreases with more distance. This is a law of physics you will soon learn in school, if you haven't already.

**Is this the way to hold a flash camera?**

**Explain what is wrong with this picture and how it can be corrected. Look for the answer at the end of this chapter.**

If you try to take a flash picture of objects or people at different distances, those closer will be brighter and those farther away will be darker. So when you use the flash, you have to compose the picture so that things are more or less the same distance from the camera.

The flash has another use in addition to providing light in place of the sun. If you take a picture of a person's face in the sun, the print will have dark shadows and it will not be a great picture, or even a good one. The flash, however, can be used to "fill-in" the shadows. Photographers call this "fill flash."

Sometimes you will want to take pictures of something—most often a person—with the light from the sun coming towards the camera. In this case, the sunlight is in back of the subject. This method can result in great pictures.

**Without the flash, the picture looks like this.**

**Use the flash and it looks like this.**

But you need to do two things: Shade the lens and use your flash to fill-in the shadow. The easiest way to shade the lens is to position the camera at a place where there is a shadow while pointing the camera at the subject in the sun. Another way is to hold the camera with one hand and shade with the other or have someone help you to provide shade.

Almost everyone who takes pictures knows that using a flash is necessary indoors. But only a few really good photographers use the flash outdoors to fill-in shadows created by the sun. Now you know the secret and this secret will help you take great pictures.

The flash won't solve everything by itself. Remember the things you have already learned: choose the format, select a point of view, compose carefully, and hold the camera steady.

**When you use a one-time camera and you are shooting inside, you need the flash. If the walls, ceiling and floor are light colored, the picture will come out better because the light from the flash bounces around.**

In this picture, the light from the sun is behind the girl. The photographer used flash. Can you imagine what the picture might have looked like without flash?

ANSWER: The girl in front is much closer to the camera than the other two children. Her face is too light and the others are too dark. When you take a flash picture of more than one person, you have to arrange them so that they are more or less the same distance from the camera.

# Chapter 10

# TELEPHOTOS

The camera you have been using until now sees things just about the same way we do. You can check on this by looking through the viewfinder. Now take the camera away. The scene looks the same, doesn't it.

If we want to see the details in something far away, we use binoculars or a telescope.

Those who have expensive cameras are able to remove one lens and replace it with another. Some more expensive cameras have a built-in telephoto lens so that you can change back and forth between it and the normal lens.

**After you buy this camera, what is the first thing you should do? For the answer, look at the end of this chapter.**

**When you use binoculars, things that are actually far away seem to be closer. A one-time telephoto camera or a camera with a telephoto lens does the same job.**

If you don't have one of these expensive cameras, you can buy a one-time camera with a built-in telephoto lens. It costs a little more than a regular one-time camera, but not too much.

The one-time telephoto camera is quite different than the regular or the flash. The one-time telephoto camera has a different lens and it also has a different kind of film.

Notice what it says about film on the regular or flash camera: ISO 400. Now look at the telephoto camera. It says, "ISO 1600!" Photographers say that the 1600 film is "faster" than the 400.

The 1600 film can take pictures when the light is ¼ as bright as the 400. You could cut the amount of light in half and then cut it in half again. The 1600 picture would come out and the 400 one would be way too dark. Photographers say that the faster film is more sensitive to light.

Are you sensitive to light? When you go from the inside to bright sun outside, do you notice how your eyes take some time to adjust? Many people wear dark glasses in the sun because their eyes are sensitive.

**Look at the lever and the small hole in front of the lens.**

Because the 1600 film is so sensitive, the camera has to have a way to cut down the light when you want to take a picture in the bright sun. The camera does it the same way our eyes do. Look at the pupil of someone's eye in a dim room. Large, isn't it? Then go outside in the bright sun and look at someone's eye. The pupil is small. This is like different sizes of pipe. A large pipe lets in a lot of water. A small one lets in less. It is the same way with light.

Look at the front of the telephoto camera. There is a little lever. Swing the lever and a small hole appears behind the lens. When the small hole is in place, less light is let into the lens.

When you swing the lever the other way, the hole goes away and more light can come in.

When you use the telephoto outside in the sun, you have to swing the lever so the hole is behind the lens.

As you read and study the directions on the telephoto camera, you will discover that it has a method for you to find out when you should have the hole behind the lens. Be sure to use the method carefully. If you don't, your pictures will come out too light or too dark.

Do you remember how close you could get with your normal camera? Either 3 or 4 feet, right?

**When you move the lever, the small hole goes away.**

If you got closer, your pictures looked fuzzy. The telephoto camera has a different lens, so the distance is different too. Things closer than 15 feet from the will be blurred or appear out of focus.

When you use a telephoto, it changes your point of view. It seems to bring you closer to the subject.

You might very well say, "Why not just move closer and use the regular camera?" There are two answers to the question.

First of all, you may not be able to move closer. What are some situations where you cannot get closer? How about at the zoo, or at a sports event, or an airplane on a runway?

What others can you think of? The telephoto lets you take certain kinds of pictures you could not take before.

**This picture was taken with the regular one-time camera.**

**This one was taken with the telephoto. Both pictures were taken from the same place.**

The other answer is that you can take pictures where the light is less bright than the sun. This is because the camera is loaded with ISO 1600 film. With this film, you can take pictures indoors with bright lights.

Take a complete roll of film of 24 pictures with your telephoto. Experiment with a number of situations. Get the film processed and study the results.

Now you know about the telephoto and what it will do. Keep one handy so that whenever you have a picture-taking situation where you need the telephoto, it will be ready to shoot.

**ANSWER: Read the directions.**

# Chapter 11

# PANORAMAS

There is another kind of one-time camera available. It is called a panoramic camera. It takes long, narrow pictures called panoramas. A panorama is a wide view of a place or thing. When you stand at the beach, or on a hill, or on a tall building, or at a canyon, you can see a long way from side to side. That is called a panorama, or panoramic view. You can get the same effect with a camera which has a wide-angle lens—it will take a picture that shows a wide view.

Remember what you learned about the telephotos? A telephoto lens is like a telescope. It brings the camera closer. A wide-angle lens is the opposite. It takes the camera farther away.

It includes more in the composition.

The panoramic camera is another, kind of camera. So be sure to read the directions carefully before you try to use it. After you take your first panoramic pictures and get your prints back, you will discover that they are a different size: 3½ inches tall and 10 inches long.

To take great pictures with your panoramic camera, you have to observe some different rules. Look at the box. What kind of film does it have? Somewhere you will see "ISO 200." What number did the package for the regular camera have? It had 400, right? Because 200 is less than 400, the 400 film is faster than the 200. Saying it backwards, the 200 film is slower than the 400.

When it came from the store, this picture was 10 inches long. It is smaller in this book because the page is not big enough.

What does this mean when we take pictures? There has to be more light to get a good photograph. The panoramic camera can only be used when the sun is out or when it is only partly cloudy. It cannot be used in the shade or when it is completely cloudy unless you use a flash.

The second important rule about the panoramic camera is that you must be extra careful about keeping it level. If you are just a little bit off, the result will be a strange-looking photograph.

There are two different ways you can tilt the camera. You could get it off level by having one side higher than the other. Or you could point it up or down.

**You can buy a panoramic camera with a flash built in. You can also buy panoramic cameras without the flash. The one with the flash costs a little more.**

**As soon as you get a panoramic camera, you will find a lot of pictures to take that would not**

With other kinds of cameras, you may point it up or down on purpose. This is okay and often results in interesting photographs. But with the panoramic, you have to be sure it is level both ways. Always point the camera straight ahead. Don't tilt it in any way.

The third rule has to do with light. When you take a panoramic picture, the sunlight should always be at your back. It doesn't have to be absolutely, directly at your back. But it has to be back there somewhere. The light from the sun cannot come from the side or the front.

Panoramic pictures only work well with certain kinds of subjects.

Can you think of what these are? Things that are long and not too tall, right? You will get an effect from a panoramic picture which is not like any other.

To take great panoramic pictures, you have to think and work a lot on the composition. There is one picture you should take with your first panoramic camera: your home. With the regular camera, you can usually only include the building you live in. With a panoramic, you can include part of the neighborhood too. This can tell a very interesting story and could become a valuable record for the future.

Please... Keep Your Beach Clean

**be as good if you had used a regular-size camera.**

If you live in a very tall building, you may want to take a vertical format panorama. This way you can include the entire building. Even if you take such a picture, take one in the horizontal format, too. Show just the bottom or entrance and include things that are on each side.

Do you remember the rule about the light when you are taking a panoramic? It must be sunlit and the sun must be at your back. When you go outside to look at your home, you may not be able to take a picture right away. What if the sunlight is coming from the back and not striking the front? You could take a picture of the back, of course, and this might be interesting. But we really want a record of how the front looks.

During every day, the direction of the sunlight changes. The sun comes up in the east and sets in the west. At different times of the year, it moves north or south. (Actually, we know that it is the earth that is rotating and tilting, not the sun.)

Look at your home many times during a day. Depending on where the sun is, it looks a little different each time. There is probably one single time when you can take a really great picture. At other times you will get an ordinary picture or even a bad picture. It all depends on where the light is coming from.

To take a satisfactory panorama, you have to find out what time of the day the sun will be at your back. The sunlight rule for a panorama has helped us learn something significant about every picture, including the ones when you are not using a panoramic camera. It is very important where the light comes from.

**Can you explain what is wrong with this picture and why? Look at the end of this chapter for the answer.**

**Most people take panoramic pictures in the horizontal format. But if you really look, you can take interesting and exciting pictures in the vertical format.**

With a panoramic camera, you can arrange interesting compositions of groups of people. With the panoramic camera for instance, you could have 12 people all sitting side by side. If you used a regular camera for this picture, you would be far away and the picture would have to include a lot you wouldn't want.

Think of some other situations where a panoramic camera could take a great picture. How about a tennis match or a basketball game? With a panoramic, you could photograph the entire court.

Because you have read the directions carefully, you know that there may be only 12 pictures on a panoramic film roll. Now that you have the camera, take all the pictures. Try to include as many different situations as possible. You need to have the experience of these pictures and you need to see the results of your efforts.

When you get the prints back, study them carefully. Some will be more successful than others. Try to figure out why. From now on, always keep a panoramic camera handy, because you never know when you will need it. If you don't have one ready to shoot, you might miss a great picture.

**ANSWER: The picture is too dark because there was not enough light. Panoramic pictures must be taken in direct sunlight or with the flash.**

## Chapter 12

# IN THE WATER

Do you remember some of the things you learned in Chapter One? What were the rules about taking care of your camera? If you said one of them is to keep it dry and don't get it wet or damp, you are right.

Most cameras can be damaged or destroyed by water. Some special cameras are waterproof. There are many cameras like this and some of them are expensive.

What is the most important thing to remember when you are playing or swimming in the water? For the answer, look at the end of this chapter.

When you go to buy a waterproof camera, be sure to check the outside of the package to make sure you have the right model. Water or any moisture will damage all of the others.

You can buy a one-time camera sealed in a plastic box to protect it from water. A camera like this is only a little more expensive than the others. It will let you take pictures you cannot get with cameras that are not waterproof.

By now, you know the very first thing to do, don't you? Read the directions. Some of the directions on the box and on the waterproof camera are the same as the others. Look to see what kind of film it has. Is it the same as any of the other cameras?

One of the directions is completely different. You can use this camera in the water. How deep can you take the camera in the water?

The directions say not more than 8 feet deep. If you take it deeper, water will probably seep in and ruin your pictures.

A waterproof camera is very useful in other ways besides when you are swimming. The camera is sealed to keep out water. It will also keep out dirt and dust. The camera is also a lot tougher than the others, so you can treat it more roughly. This does not mean, however, that it will not break, because it will.

**When you take pictures in places like this, you will want to use the waterproof camera even though you don't take any photographs under water.**

**With a waterproof camera, you will soon be taking shots like this. With the wide-angle lens, you have to position yourself closer to your subjects.**

The water-proof camera has another feature you may want to take advantage of. It has a wider-angle lens than does the regular or the flash cameras. Do you remember our discussion of wide-angle lenses in the panoramic camera chapter? A wide-angle lens is the opposite of a telescope or a telephoto lens. It includes more than a normal lens.

Before you start to use the waterproof camera, check to see just how different the wide-angle lens is than the normal lens on the regular and flash cameras.

To see the difference, hold a regular camera directly on top of a waterproof camera. Look in one viewfinder and then the other. Notice the things you can see in one viewfinder and not in the other. The waterproof camera sees almost twice as much as do the others.

Can you think of the reason for the wide-angle lens in the waterproof camera? Have you ever dived under the water with goggles or a mask? You can't see very far, can you? When you take pictures under water, you have to get much closer to your subjects.

Some people use a waterproof because it has a wide-angle lens. For this reason, the camera is useful even if you never get it wet.

A camera with a wide-angle lens allows you to take pictures which might not otherwise have been possible.

Peter Gowland

**When you go to the beach, or to a water park, it is a good idea to take along a waterproof camera.**

**To check the difference in lenses, hold the regular model on top of the waterproof, then compare what you see in each viewfinder.**

**The wide-angle lens on the waterproof camera includes more in the picture. For this reason, you may want to always have a waterproof camera with you.**

**ANSWER: Never swim alone.**

# Chapter 13

# YOUR NEIGHBORHOOD

Now that you know how to take pictures, what should you take pictures of? Among the most important are things or people we want to remember. Another good reason to shoot is to communicate with someone else. And photographs make great gifts because they are very personal.

To take great pictures, you need to practice. Practicing photography is done in a certain way. First you shoot, next you get the film processed and printed and then you study the results. As you study the results, you say to yourself: "What could I have done to have made a better picture?"

Many times in photography, you can shoot the same thing over again and make improvements. A wise photographer once said, "One of the most important differences between a good photographer and a bad one is that a good photographer always throws bad photographs away and never lets anyone see them."

Every photographer makes mistakes. You will too. Expect it. Not every single picture taken by even the very best photographers is great. If you take 10 pictures of your best friend or your pet or your mother, one will be better than the rest. In fact, one may be great, a few so-so and the rest bad. One rule for taking great pictures is, throw the rest away.

Don't show them to anyone unless that someone is an expert and you want his or her opinion.

Another way to get a great picture is to keep trying. Take the same thing over and over again until you get it right. To make this easy, start taking pictures in your own neighborhood. This way, the subjects will still be there.

What are the photo subjects in your neighborhood? The photographs that will mean the most to you in the future are those of people. Your family members are now and will probably always be the most important people in your life. Take pictures of them. Next, you'll want to take pictures of your friends and neighbors.

**Why do you think these dolls are good subjects to practice with? The answer is at the end of this chapter.**

Animals are often important in our lives. Some animals become our very good friends. Do you have a pet: a dog, a cat, or a bird? Some people have more than one pet. Usually a pet will not live as long as you will. Dogs and cats rarely live more than 20 years and most a lot less. So the pet you have today may not be with you always. But you'll want to remember. Today, if you think about your pet, you can create an image of what the pet looks like in your mind. But after your pet is no longer with you and time passes, creating the image will be harder and harder. A photograph is a wonderful way to remember a pet.

There are all sorts of other things to take pictures of in your home and your neighborhood. Can you think of some things that you may want to remember in the future? How about your mom cooking in the kitchen? How about your own room, or the places you play?

What about your best friend's home? Is there a park nearby? There are all sorts of picture opportunities in parks.

Do you know what a portrait is? A portrait is a picture of a person. Many portraits are photographs, but some are paintings or drawings. Many of the greatest works of art are portraits. The next time you are in your school or public library, ask the librarian to show you where you can find books with examples of great art. Look at portraits and study what the artist was doing.

If you can learn to take really good portraits, you will be a better photographer than most people who own cameras. Start out by practicing on someone close to you. The best subject is a brother, sister or friend.

Your regular one-time camera is a good one to start taking portraits with. You don't need one with the flash or anything else.

**Sometimes exciting things happen in your neighborhood. It's a good idea to have a camera ready and handy.**

Do you remember the directions about light? You have to take pictures in sunlight, on a cloudy day or in the shade when the sun is out. If you take a picture of a person with the sun hitting the face, the results will not be great. So you should take portraits in the shade. The shade can be provided by clouds or by some object.

To take a portrait, get a chair or stool for your subject to sit on. The lighter the chair or stool, the better, so you can move it around easily. Many photographers like to use a stool rather than a chair so the back of the chair doesn't show in the picture.

Find a good place to take your pictures. The place should be as bright as possible, but not in the sun. Bushes and trees don't usually make good shade. Little spots of sunlight may come through and spoil your even shade.

**After you have read all of this chapter, why not try a portrait of a relative or a friend? Use your 3 or 4 foot stick to make sure you have your camera at the closest possible distance. Take the picture in open shade when the sun is out or on a bright, overcast day.**

**Kids and pets together can be the subjects for you take great pictures. There are usually plenty around in most neighborhoods.**

Next, select a background. The background should not be sunny or even partly sunny. Bushes and plants don't usually make good backgrounds. It is often best if the background is darker than your subject.

Put the stool down and have your subject sit on it. Hold your camera between 4 and 5 feet from your subject's face. An easy way to help measure is with a 4-foot stick. Keep the stick nearby and hold it between your camera and the subject.

Your portrait will be better if your camera is a little higher than your subject's face, and tilted down.

Move the stool around until you like the look of the background. Check the background in your viewfinder. Should you use a horizontal or a vertical format? Think about the things you learned about composition.

When you take a portrait there is something else to think about. Can you tell what that is? What can make the difference between a good portrait and a bad one?

Unless you are shooting for school ID cards or driver's licenses, the idea of a portrait is to capture your subject's personality. How do you do this? For one thing, study the face. Our faces are mirrors of our personalities. If you can only capture a certain expression, you can record what sort of person this is.

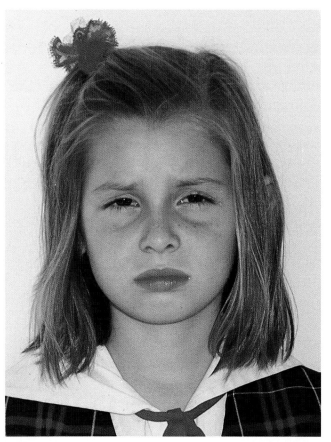

**What do you think of this portrait? What would you do to make it better? How would you do it?**

Taking portraits takes patience. Many people feel uncomfortable when they are having their pictures taken. Your job is to put them at ease. Your subject should be relaxed and happy. You may have to keep talking while you are taking pictures.

A good way to get people to feel at ease and happy is to get them to talk about themselves. Ask questions. Don't ask yes or no questions. Say, "Tell me about your train set. What have you added to it lately?" Or, "What are your plans for summer vacation?" While they talk, keep looking at the face. When you see the expression you want, say, "Stop, don't move." Then squeeze off your shot.

Don't expect to take a great or even a good portrait with only one shot. You may have to take quite a few. Some people take an entire roll to get one good portrait. And the best thing about your first portrait is that you can get the film processed, study the results and do it all over again.

People aren't the only ones in the neighborhood you can take portraits of. How about pets? If you have a pet, your next assignment is to take a pet portrait. Use the same techniques: Shoot in the shade, watch the background, put the pet on a stool or something high and talk while you shoot. This is often a lot harder than shooting people. Your pet may get tired of sitting there and run away. Or it may want to jump on you. This takes a lot of patience, but you will end up with a portrait to treasure for your entire life.

**ANSWER: Pick a subject to practice on that you can go back and take over and over again. These dolls are right at home, always waiting patiently.**

# Chapter 14

# SHOOT A PARTY

Everyone who has a camera shoots parties. More photographs are taken at parties than for any other purpose.

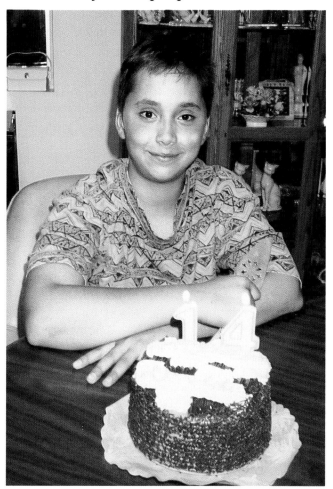

**A birthday person with the cake is a standard party picture. You should learn to do them well. What could you have done to make this picture better? For the answer, look at the end of this chapter.**

Because you have already shot at least a few rolls of film, you may have tried to shoot a party. This book has a separate chapter on shooting parties because doing a good job is not that easy. Because you have been studying this book, you may have been taking some pretty good pictures; maybe even a few great ones. So your family and friends may expect a lot from you when you shoot a party.

Party pictures are the kind of pictures your family and friends will want copies of. You can learn a few professional tricks and not let them down. Some professional photographers—those who shoot weddings, for instance—make their livings shooting parties. The pictures have to be good or no one will pay for them.

If the party is indoors or at night, you will have to use a flash camera. Before you start to shoot, review the flash chapter (9) and read the directions again. You should be very sure of yourself when you shoot a party. Even if the party is outdoors in the sun, you may want to use the flash camera so that the people pictures in the sun will come out great.

What are the important things about the flash camera? Before you can shoot, you have to push the flash button and wait for the ready light. You can't shoot anything that is more than 10 feet away.

**Good un-posed or candid shots are often harder to take than the ones where everyone is still and looking into the camera.**

sure each face is in the picture.

When you have the group together, make sure everyone can see the camera. If they can't see the camera, the camera can't see them.

Think about a background. A plain light or medium colored wall is often the best. If you are inside and using a flash and there is a great distance between your subjects and the background, it will turn out very dark or black. A black background is not pleasing. If you are doing a group, you may have to move people and

What are the other things?

If they are not in your head, read Chapter 9 one more time. This time, make a list.

One of the pictures we take all the time at parties are group shots. There are two kinds: posed and un-posed. Both can be difficult and the more people, the harder it is. The big problem is the expressions on people's faces. Great expressions equal great pictures and vice versa.

When you take a portrait of one person, all you have to think about is the expressions on one face. When you take a group, you have to consider each face. The first thing to do is make

**Your party pictures may be more interesting if the people in them are doing something.**

**Look at this picture carefully. Can you see everyone's face clearly? With such a large group, you may have to take a number of shots to get a good picture.**

things around to get the best effect.

Do you remember what you learned about the light from the flash? If you have something close and another farther away, the close thing will be too bright and the farther one too dark. Because of this, you have to try to arrange a group of people so that their faces are more or less the same distance from your camera. There are all sorts of ways to do this and the best solution often depends on the number of people and the occasion. This is much easier to do with a posed group.

One way to improve your group shots is to study how others have solved the problem. Look in magazines that have a lot of people pictures. There will probably be quite a number of group shots. These will have been taken by professionals. When you find examples you think you can use, cut them out and make your own scrap book. Then, the next time you get ready to shoot a party, study your scrap book. Every time you find a good example, add to it.

After you have made sure you have included each face in your viewfinder, you have to work on the expressions. One way to ruin a group picture is to have some people with their eyes closed. The more people, the more likely you are to get one with eyes closed. The only solution to this

**Parties on special days like Halloween should be recorded with photographs. Try to get interesting or fun expressions on everyone's face.**

is to shoot more than one picture. Three pictures is better for a group.

Parties are supposed to be happy times. So you'll want happy expressions on the faces in your groups. A trick many people use is to have everyone say, "cheese." This may be corny, but it works. Maybe a better way is to tell a little joke. One liners are best.

Great pictures result from great compositions. Just standing a group of people in a row is pretty ordinary, isn't it? There are all sorts of ways you can arrange a group of people. They don't all have to stand. Some can sit. Others can kneel. And there are different ways to stand, sit and kneel. Use your imagination and try to do something different. Shoot your group on stairs or shoot straight down. Be daring. Experiment. If it doesn't work, throw it away. You learn from things that don't work, as well as things that do work.

Parties happen only one time. There may be another party with the same people, but it will be different. A party is not like the things and people you were shooting in the neighborhood. You can't go back and shoot it again.

The way a professional shoots a party is to buy insurance. The insurance is to take a lot of pictures. If you have a party and you shoot only one picture and it doesn't come out, you don't have any remembrance of the party. For one reason or another, lots of pictures may not come out. Only a few may be great. The way to buy insurance at a party is to shoot a lot.

**ANSWER: The background is cluttered and doesn't add anything interesting. A plain wall would have been better. If the cake were positioned closer to the boy and if his arms were not on the table, the "14" would stand out better against his shirt.**

# Chapter 15

# VACATIONS AND TRIPS

If people take the most pictures at parties and celebrations, vacations and trips come in a close second. When on a trip or vacation, almost everyone takes pictures. Some take only a few while others take hundreds.

Now that you have advanced this far, when you go on your next trip or take a vacation, you will want to take pictures too. If you have read this book carefully and taken pictures as you went along, you now know more about photography than most people. Are your new skills showing up in the quality of your pictures? Probably so. When you take your next trip, your family and friends will expect a lot.

Shooting pictures on trips and vacations is like photographing other subjects. If you can get in some practice, you will do better on the real thing. A good time to practice is when you are on a one-day trip.

Whenever you go on a trip, take your camera along. Before you leave, be sure you have everything you need. If you are camping in the woods, there may not be a nearby store.

**Does this picture tell a story? For the answer, look at the end of this chapter.**

Do you have activities on weekends? Do you ever go to the zoo, or an amusement park? Even a visit to a swap meet qualifies. The next time you go, take your camera and practice.

Shooting a trip is not like taking pictures in your own neighborhood. A successful trip requires planning. What will you need to take along with you? You will want to take the things you will need, but not any more. If you take too much, you will be loaded down like a pack mule and you won't have much fun.

An important place to start is with a camera bag. You don't need a fancy one.

Just something to hold your stuff. A camera bag should have a strap so you can carry it on your shoulder and have your hands free to handle your camera. After you have the things you are going to take all together, get the smallest bag you can find that will hold everything.

Most camera stores have a choice of a large variety of camera bags. Discount, variety and drugstores usually have bags too. Your bag should not only carry your things, but also protect them. Bags with some kind of padding are good. Then if you hit the bag against something hard, the things inside won't break. If your bag is not well padded, you can make some padding out of sponge rubber. Sponge rubber can be cut with a sharp knife or scissors.

What are some of the things you will want to take? Obviously your camera. If you use one-time cameras, depending on where you are going and how long you are going to stay, you may want to take more than one camera. And you may want to consider taking one or more of the different kinds of one-time cameras. Even if you don't plan on going in the water, the wide-angle lens in the waterproof may come in handy.

But if you are going to a place like Disneyland, you don't have to take along a lot of one-time cameras. You can buy them there.

**This is a picture of the famous California mission at San Juan Capistrano. It has been photographed thousands of times, but only you can take a picture like this. Why?**

Of course, you may want to consider the price. Things like cameras and film are almost always more expensive at an amusement park or vacation spot. If you are going camping, there may not be any stores nearby and you will have to take everything.

Planning includes finding out exactly where you are going and what you will be doing. For example, if you are going boating, you will want to take along a waterproof. There is a lot of spray in the air when you go in a small, open boat. This much dampness could damage a regular camera.

When you are on a trip, what do you think are the important things to shoot?

Would you say buildings, mountains, statues or people? If you were to take a trip to Washington, D.C., you would probably go to see the Lincoln Memorial. It is one of the most famous places in Washington and almost everyone who visits there goes to see it.

When you get to the Lincoln Memorial, you will want to take a picture so you will remember your visit. What kind of a picture do you think you would want? Would you take a picture of the statue alone? How many times do you think someone has taken a picture of the statue of Lincoln? Among many others, professionals have shot it too. Do you think you can do it better?

**If the two boys were your relatives, which of these pictures would you want to keep to show your friends and your children and grandchildren when you have them?**

What can you do to make your picture different? What can you do to make it important to you and your family? The answer is to include someone with whom you are traveling. It could be someone in your family or a friend. Of course, this idea is not new. Lots of people include someone important to them in a picture like this. Your job is to think of a way to compose the picture in an interesting and even artistic way.

When you are on a trip, the most important subjects for you to take pictures of are people. The buildings, statues, bridges, waterfalls and mountains have all been photographed before. If you want a picture of the Lincoln Memorial, you can buy postcards.

Probably, they will have a much better picture than you can take yourself.

The people you will want to include are not only those who are traveling with you, but also those you may meet along the way. The best travel pictures are those that look as if they are natural. Pictures of an historic building with your mother or friend just standing in front are not very interesting. Study what people do. Then take pictures that include an activity. Maybe it's just talking with someone else. You may have to direct them in order to get a great picture.

**ANSWER: Notice what is in the background. Now you know where they are.**

# Chapter 16

# ALBUMS AND SUCH

By now, you probably have a lot of pictures. There are a number of things you can do with them. Most families have albums of photographs. You will want to start one of your very own.

An album can be like a diary. You can record the important things that happen to you in an album. Do your parents have albums? Do your grandparents? Take a look at them. Can you imagine how wonderful it will be to have your own albums to show your own grandchildren?

While many people put their pictures in albums, some just leave them in the envelopes they came in or have them around here and there. This is too bad. If they are kept in the original envelopes, they are not very handy to look at. If they are left lying around, they will probably be lost sooner or later.

There is another reason for putting them away: If color prints are left in the light, eventually they will fade. And, over time, all of the picture will go away leaving a blank, white piece of paper. Also when color prints are left in the light too long, the colors will slowly change. These are good reasons for keeping your negatives in a safe place.

Look in your parents' or grandparents' albums. Are there pictures of their parents and grandparents? Are all of the pictures identified? Do you know who each person is?

**Does your family have a photo album? Maybe you will want to start one just for yourself.**

Do you know when and where each photo was taken? Maybe you can ask your parents or grandparents and they can tell you.

Give yourself a test. Without any help from anyone, can you look at a photograph and identify your grandparents parents or grandparents? And how about uncles and cousins?

Identification is very important for the value the pictures will have in the future.

Make it a habit to identify your prints as soon as you get them back. On the back of each print, write the date and place where the picture was taken plus the name and relationship of each person. You cannot write on the back of a print with a pencil or ordinary pen. You will have to use a marker. After you have written the identification, be sure to let the marker ink dry before you do anything with the prints.

One way to organize an album is by date. This way, an album tells the story of the progress of a family or the life of an individual. Some have a family album plus separate albums for each family member.

There are other ways to organize albums. For instance, if you take an important trip, you may want to tell the story of the trip in a separate album. You may want to create your own personal school yearbook. Some people collect pictures they have taken of birds or animals. The possibilities are endless.

Before you start, you will have to pick out the type of album to use. There are many different ways of putting pictures in albums. You will want to pick out the one you think will be the best for you.

To do this, go to a camera or variety store and look at all the different types available. Some are more expensive than others, so you may want to think about the price too.

Some of the most interesting albums are those in which there is a combination of pictures and writing. Of course, you have already written the identification on the back of each print. But you can't read what is there without taking the print out of the album. This is not very handy. Every album tells a story in one way or another. But the story may not be obvious to everyone who looks at it. And you may forget parts of the story as time goes by.

One way to do this is to write a caption for each picture. What should you write on the captions?

**Photos can be displayed in all sorts of interesting ways. This one includes a picture of each of the kids in a family on their first day of kindergarten.**

Answer these questions: Who? What? When? Where? Why? How? How Many? How Much? Take one of the pictures you have just taken and practice writing a caption. Show it to your mother and get her opinion of how you did. If you have a typewriter or computer and can type, you will want to type your captions.

This way, your album will look neat and professional. Everyone will be able to read it too!

There are other things you can do with your pictures. For one thing, they make excellent gifts, especially the portraits. When you give a photograph as a gift, you will want to get an enlargement. You can order enlargements at the same store where you get your pictures processed. The usual sizes are 5 by 7 inches, 8 by 10 inches and 11 by 14 inches.

Most stores have a display of the different choices. Here is something to take into consideration before you spend money on an enlargement: The larger the enlargement, the more noticeable your mistakes. If a small print looks not quite sharp, when you make an enlargement it will be very fuzzy. A good idea is to study a print with a magnifying glass before you have an enlargement made.

When you give a gift, you won't want to just give the print alone. It makes a much nicer gift if you put the print in a frame or folder.

**This is a traditional photo greeting card.**

This is one side of a postcard made from a photograph.

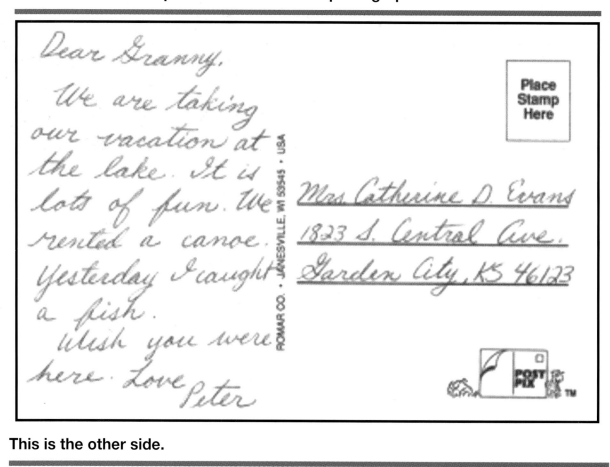

Dear Granny,
    We are taking our vacation at the lake. It is lots of fun. We rented a canoe. Yesterday I caught a fish.
    Wish you were here. Love, Peter

ROMAR CO. • JANESVILLE, WI 53545 • USA

Mrs Catherine D Evans
1823 S. Central Ave.
Garden City, KS 46123

Place Stamp Here

POST PIX ™

This is the other side.

Many different types of stores sell all sorts of frames and folders. A frame need not be expensive. Discount stores usually have some for just a few dollars. You may even find some on sale for less than a dollar each.

Some photographs make better gifts if they are autographed or there is a message written right on the picture itself. For example, you may want to take a picture of your grandmother to give to your mother on her birthday. In this case, you may want to ask your grandmother to write a message of love on the print.

Pencils and most pens do not write very well on photographs. Some markers will write on prints, but usually you can wipe off the writing very easily.

The best way to solve this problem is to go to an art supply or stationery store and buy a special pen called a paint pen. A paint pen is made like a can of spray paint. You shake it up before you write with it. Paint pens come in various widths and many colors. Pick out the paint pen that suits your picture.

Another way to give a photograph as a gift is to send it as a postcard. Many stores that have pictures processed sell 4 by 6 inch postcard blanks. One side is like any other postcard: There is a place for the stamp, the address and the message. On the other side is glue protected by paper. To make a picture postcard, you strip away the protective paper and stick down your photograph.

CHRISTMAS 91                                    ALICE & PETER

**Cards can be humorous too. This is a card from the famous photographer Peter Gowland and his wife Alice.**

Many people send photographs as Christmas cards or on other occasions when they send greeting cards. Have you ever seen a card which includes a photograph? Usually the photograph is a picture of the family, children or pets. It could be anything. When you shoot for a card, try to find a subject which is important to you or your family.

Why not give this a try yourself? Take a picture which will become your family's holiday card. Cards for personalized photographs are sold in most camera stores and some other types of stores that sell cameras, film and processing.

Do you like posters? Lots of kids collect posters of sports heroes, movie stars or musicians and hang them on their bedroom walls. You can have posters made from your own photographs. They are not as expensive as you may think. The next time you go to a camera store, check it out. The poster prints come in various sizes with the larger ones being more expensive. A poster is nothing more than a huge enlargement. So be very sure of the quality of your picture before you have it made into a poster.

There are many other things you can do with photographs. Old-fashioned heart-shaped lockets with a picture inside make valued gifts for mothers, aunts and girlfriends. You can buy these in jewelry and department stores. Some specialty shops will print your photograph on a T-shirt. This is fun and makes a great gift for just about anyone.

Photography is an important hobby. It helps all of us to keep a record of our lives. It is also a profession. There are many jobs in the photographic industry. Actually, there are more than 100 specialties. Hundreds of thousands of people are employed in photography. If you really enjoyed this book and taking pictures, maybe you will want to consider the profession of photography.

Peter Gowland